God's Special Educators Are Teachers Too

*An Alphabet Soup Bowl
in a Book of A-Z Poetic
Inspirations for Teachers*

Jeanine Jones

Speak To Me

Speak To Me Books
Memphis, TN

God's Special Educators are Teachers Too
An Alphabet Soup Bowl in a Book of A-Z Poetic
Inspirations for Teachers: Volume 2

Copyright © 2018 by Jeanine Jones, Speak To Me Books

Paperback ISBN: 978-0-9884394-3-6
Ebook ISBN: 978-0-9884394-4-3

Credits: Teaching Standards 1-7 are from the Shelby County Schools Teacher Effectiveness Measurement Tool

Cover Design: Tywebbin Creations

DEDICATION

For
All of God's Special Teachers

Especially,
Gina S. Harkness
the most special teacher I knew.
R.I.P.

ACKNOWLEDGEMENTS

Thank you, God, for allowing me to express myself poetically. Thank you, Marcus, my husband and biggest cheerleader for believing in me, being patient and always taking care of home. My children, I thank you for riding along with me on this journey. Lastly, but never least, I acknowledge and am thankful for my dearest friend, the late great, Gina S. Harkness, for always supporting me when most discounted me.

CONTENTS

INTRODUCTION

Working in education is arguably the most difficult profession. Why one chooses it can be questionable. Survey several educators and ask them why they chose teaching as a career. Surely, you will get several different answers. Ask them why they stay, the same thing. Ask them why they chose Special Education and they might cry. However, all of the questions answered will have some hint of "I wanted to make a difference" in the response.

You are making a difference, even when you think that you are not. As educators, many find themselves in the depths of the valley at some point of their careers. The work gets harder year after year. The pay gets funnier year after year, and you get tired, year after year.

You have invested in the academic journey that is for the most part, a thankless job. Get out if you need to. But if you intend to keep fighting on the frontline, stay equipped and refreshed. Meanwhile, throughout the school year, periodically, sip on *God's Special Educators are Teachers Too*, a **heartfelt, humorous** alphabet soup bowl in a book. It is a special recipe cooked up just for you in one big poetic pot of a greeting card, if you will, to inspire you on your journey. Enjoy it!

Have a great school year!
Jeanine Jones
#teachon

Jeanine Jones

Special Education
An Acrostic Introduction

Superior...

As a special education teacher, you support students, families and co-teachers. Becoming an advocate for the student and her unique learning style, you plan a program in the best interest of the child's growth. You fight for students to participate in extracurricular activities, general education classes, support/encore and elective courses. You make sure the parents and guardians understand the plan and address their concerns. Co-teachers share insight on students' present levels of performance. Administrators sign off on the Individualized Education Program (IEP) and "make sure you are in compliance".

You're the staple and rarity in the building. You're deemed as the reading specialist, behavior specialist, compliance specialist, and reading and behavior interventionists. The way you run around to get things done is unbelievable.

You do all of this and still you are evaluated with the same Teacher Effective Measure (TEM)rubric as the general education teacher and receive the same salary. Expected to deliver objective driven lessons, explain content, provide appropriately challenging work, maintain content engagement, teach higher level thinking skills, check for understanding and make the most of instructional time, all while writing several IEPs, that all require several professionals and parents that you have to gather to meet and agree on what is best for said child.

You are superior for the latter alone.

Professional growth and learning, use of data, school and community environment, and leadership comes with the territory of being a special education teacher.

Protector...

Protector of files
confidentiality
records
students
rights

and your sanity

protecting and serving
is what you do

At times you feel
less like a teacher
and more like
the secret service
or the police

Enthusiastic...

A happy face greets
your colleagues and kids
as you prepare for
another great day
of teaching and learning

You bring an enthusiastic attitude to the building
cheerful about the smallest things
keen
passionate
excited

Hoping you can
get Johnny to read
on the next level
even if it's only
site words

Caring...

You do the work
because you care
wanting the best
for students
loving them enough
to teach them
tending to their education
kindly minding the garden
of our future generation

Interesting...

Intriguing
and downright appealing
believe it or not
some people are in awe
of what you do

your work is noteworthy
although, some think
you just sit in your classroom
coat closet or makeshift office all day
looking at a computer screen
or shuffling papers
twiddling your thumbs
waiting on your special students
to come

they wonder
what it would be like
to twiddle their thumbs too
trying to figure out
how you do
what you do
they inquire
trying to figure you

so, you give them a crash course
in SPED 101
admiring you more for
your ability to maintain
in a branch of the profession
that has literally driven some insane
they quickly appreciate their positions
and stay in their lanes

Special Education
is not for everyone
just the special people

God's Special Educators Are Teachers Too

I mean, the very special people

Artsy...

You love the arts
theatre, music, visual arts

this comes as no surprise
so does your kids

a huge arts integrationist
you teach using the arts

your kids are painting this and that
rapping, dancing, and making beats

You make a poem
or a pneumonic for
every lesson
every week
challenging the artistic side of them
they compose songs, write poetry
and perform poetry slams
they start to believe in themselves
and buy into
being artsy, because
being artsy is them
being artsy is smart and
being artsy has always been in

Liberal...

Making a substantial contribution
to education
nontraditional and liberated

generously, sharing your ideas
and opinions
about how education should look
how it should be

free-thinking
is how you teach your students
to think

progressive ahead of your time
enlightening the head of the class
making him aware of his shine

Exceptional...

Exceptional
like the challenged students
you serve
there is nothing ordinary
about you
Incomparable
to anyone else
in the school

Determined...

You're determined
to plan all meetings
conduct them
get signatures
send off faxes
check files
and teach the objective
so students reach
their annual goal(s)

Upstanding...

Upstanding
doing what is right
as an educator of students
with special needs
demanding fairness
regardless of his disability
exhibiting integrity in all you do
strong and honorable
is the teacher in you

Case Managers...

Case managers
with a mountain of paper work
that never goes down
managing IEP meetings and case-loads
can get overwhelming
the tremendous amount of stress
is overpowering at times
the key is to retreat
pulling back
from it all
until you can get ahold
of the puzzle pieces
of special education
that happen to be your livelihood
brainstorming how you can tackle
the current situation
without being tackled
and developing the best possible outcome
for the student
is the next step
to cracking the case

Advocators...

Being the biggest advocate
for the child
you make sure
their special needs are met

As an activist
believer and education promoter
you listen to the input
from all stakeholders
regarding the student
determining what is best

all while teaching
campaigning and advocating
you remain the advocate and
teacher at large
with the child's best interest
at heart

Tolerant...

Tolerating little pay
long work days
budget cuts and delays
patiently, shifting the mold
for change
for you know
it is coming

continuing your teaching journey

easy going
most mischief is tolerable
even in zero zones

in your practice

you have mastered
"the patience of Job"

your lenient smiles
of encouragement
steer little ones in your presence
to make strong choices

forgiving your scholars
like God forgives all

accepting them
for who they are
their differences
their levels
their styles

open-minded
granting forbearance
giving second
and beyond third chances

until you reach
your daily max
offering clean slates
to everyone the very next day

Innovative...

Coming up with new ideas
is your thing
creative to the highest degree
groundbreaking
advanced state of the art inventions
new strategies and technologies
to help define

students' intentions
freedom forward
thinking beyond
the next graduating class
surpassing
2025
creating lexile wars
innovatively, you plan ahead
for them to defeat
their top scores

Over-the –Top…

OTT
excessive
dramatic
theatrical
overemotional
is the new Special
OTT the new diagnosis and label
for the over the top
Special Educator …

New-Normal…

Everywhere you look
school systems are looking for
special education teachers
they are paying for their classes and certification
sticking them in classes by the minute

we are all special educators
like our students
we all just
have not been identified

God's Special Educators Are Teachers Too

SPED is the New Normal
SNN - since we have abbreviations
for everything

general education teachers
are joining us in
the never-ending marathon
the one without
a finish line
they are teaching letter sounds, phonics and fluency
to upper grades
basic math and social skills...

considering all this
it is quite possible
that in some schools
half of the scholars served
would or could qualify for an IEP
some of us teachers too

to unleash creativity

and not focus on the original thought of education
working in factories
or the latter, A.C.T's, or S.A.T's
but focus on what the creator
created us to be

individual and unique
thinking freely
out of the box
not always
connecting the dots
coloring out of the lines
to make art
to do something
that has never been done
avoiding or embracing the new norm

Jeanine Jones

A-M Poetic Inspiration for God's Special Educator

Amazing...

You are amazing!
two snaps, thumbs up, and a clap amazing
through years of teaching
nothing comes to your surprise

but you always seem to surprise
with your amazing talents
and accomplishments
tackling every conundrum
that comes before your eyes

invoking wisdom and drive
sparking growth
one objective at a time

shocking all with admirable results
pushing students towards
various vocations and professions
you often leave all in amazement

Benevolent...

Benign to petty problems
compassionately, cutting out
classroom chaos
kindheartedly

making a difference, altruistically
filled with benevolence
selflessly giving back
through philanthropic
noble and humane teaching

through your kindness
you remain a constant in education
instilling and maintaining
a much-needed love
for learning

Cheerful...

Cheering on your students
from the first day of kindergarten
to the last day of college
you're their biggest cheerleader

your cheerful personality
makes you approachable
and gets students ready for learning

from one-minute math stints
to the weekly reader challenges
corralling pep rallies for
excellent behavior, parties and tests

your school spirit
is unmatched
you have the school jacket, hat, t-shirt
seat cushion, mug
and water bottle to match
displaying school pride
with the spirit
of the school mascot
that you can't hide

Rah, Rah, Rah! Hurrah, Hurrah!

teacher/cheerleader
you make learning
an enjoyable ride

Deserving...

Deserving of every teacher perk
paycheck and then some
retailer discounts and all things
teacher fun
because you are totally awesome
just for doing what you do

Education...

earning bachelors, and beyond
masters and doctorate degrees
as an educator, possibly, the most educated
lending your education to all professions, careers
vocations, and trades

education is your mantra
for you know it is key to
opening paths of possibility

through schooling and tutoring
you show scholars which road to take
with the many decisions they must make
the instruction you give
helps them discern and understand things
for their own edification

under your tutelage
from the deep roots
of green grass
to the oceans
of never-ending blue skies
an educated
culture rises

Flexible...

As an educator...
flexibility is the bible
that you are well versed in

physically and mentally
getting around rambunctious kids
every second
wrapping your mind around
the ever changing
order of the day

cutting through the red tape
to pull things that make no sense
together

stretched to the most maxed degree
you remain flexible
through assemblies
clubs
announcements
unannounced
and announced observations
cafeteria
and bus duty

flexing your teaching muscles
like Gumby

getting the hard work done

remembering....

flexibility has always been
the educators winning sport

Gifted...

Catering to those that are gifted
and not-so-gifted

you realize that gifted
is a disability too
teaching the Clue
Creative Learning Unique Environment scholars
and the clueless
giving it your best shot

those little high achieving wiz kids
sometimes know more than you
and they want too run the room

occasionally, let them
according to Bill Gates
they may be your boss one day

those on the other end of the spectrum
who may or may not be
so academically inclined
are artists and creators, musical geniuses, and inventors
you recognize the individual gifts in them all
determining what God knew

all the time
they are all gifted
and for the many gifts
you share and lavish upon them
so are you

Jeanine Jones

Heroic...

In the current times
of today
bravely walking in schools
in classes fearlessly
heroically saving lives through
literacy, discipline and a genuine love for what you do

although safety first is your motto
teaching is your priority
continuously striving
 to conquer ignorance and illiteracy
for you know
it is most dangerous

you are the children's champion
a super hero
super human

Individualized...

You know that every child
is different
just as every teacher is
you are wise to individualize
all that you can

although it takes more time
and more work
from your perspective
every child
is worth it

you put in the effort surely
in part because of your job title
but mostly, because you are a teacher
who cares

Jeanine Jones

Jolly-Like-Christmas...

Decorating your class with jingle bells, trees minus the
mistletoes
you push students to set next semester's goals

Jolly-like-Christmas
with your Christmas mug
filled with coffee or tea
whichever has the most caffeine
passing out cookies, cups and cakes
among other sugary treats
after the test you always eat

Rewards, Rewards, Rewards
praise, presents, gifts, tricks and trinkets
anything to uplift

poetry, prose and sing-alongs, carols and candy canes
pepper mint sticks dipped in hot cocoa
anything to butter them up
before you feed them
what you really want them to know

incognito writing assignment in tow
using inference from the text
to predict what happens next
fills the handmade greeting cards

celebrating every accomplishment
through it all
you are celebrated
in this Jolly-like-Christmas season

Knowledgeable...

Knowledgeable about what's coming
down the turn pike
next semester
you get a head start
taking a PD hike
to make the second half of the year
better

minding test scores and percentiles
fine tooth combing
a plan for every child
well-informed expert
you know it all too well

the power of knowledge
smarts and
intelligence vs. ignorance
intelligence
always wins

giving the keys
to knowledge
unlocking the doors
to a world of opportunity

Literacy is Life, Live! ...

Literally, you are the life of the class
without you
there is no school
no lunch, no recess, no lesson
no literacy

Literacy is Life, Live!
is your sacred hymn
knowing that you can't put a price on it
and compare it to the pop culture kid craze
but for the lesson purposes
you do it anyway
hypothetically, statistically speaking
you compare stats

Price of the latest video game $700
Price of the latest cell phone $500
Price of the latest Sneakers $100

the gift of literacy...
Priceless

you give the gift of literacy daily
giving others life
a valuable tool to live

deliberately making the literate
the deliberate literate

Motivator...

Motivating minds to move pass
average thoughts and thinking

encouraging students to be better
than they were the day before
to rise to excellence on all occasions

building the mountain of knowledge
to its highest peak

preparing others to climb
as tall as trees
and stand just as firm

inspiring small hills to grow
and learn

Jeanine Jones

God's Special Educators Are Teachers Too

God's special educators are teachers too
often seen as the underdog
you are rarely captured
in the limed spotlight
you support and protect the rights
of the most vulnerable scholars
constantly advocating and writing plans
to improve his quality of life
and activities of daily living

Special education teachers are teachers too
they teach and do just as much
as the general-ed teacher
and more

often times, deemed as the in-school babysitter
her job description and work load, begs to differ

Super teacher
Superheroes
collaborate on a regular with the counselor, gen-ed-
teacher, school psychologist social worker, hearing
specialist and speech pathologist

diagnosing and proposing
a variety of services

God's Special Educators Are Teachers Too

from extended school year
to the appropriate amount of hours serviced
to pre-vocational and observation checklists
progress monitoring and benchmarking progress
you're the expert in analyzing and interpreting data
managing and filing papers

God's special educator
is like no other

Sure all God's teachers are going to heaven
but the special-ed teacher has
golden wings
that she uses on earth
to complete her many tasks

no cape
no Genie in-a-bottle magic
you just take action

no matter what they say
about what's in your styrofoam cup
coffee, tea or other
you get the job done
Super teacher
Superhero

God's special educators are teachers too
with intrinsic super powers

knocking out, not one, not two, but three IEP's
in a single day
getting all the signatures and having everyone that signed
present, in attendance, and accounted for

always putting the scholar first
you've already rehearsed the script
pre-thought the minutes and prior written notice
because you know the child
and you've got this

tracking down students throughout the day
and the scores they made
trying to keep up
as you often lose time
that seems to never be on your side
that seems to never be on your side

tackling emails, monthly meetings
teaching anywhere you can
from stair wells
to hallways
to prayer closets and conference rooms
offices and other teachers' classrooms

teaching multi-grade levels
keeping up with student's gen-ed assignments, grades
schedules and lunch periods
psychological evaluations and re-evals
you experience the greatest level of frustration and stress

you continue to give pep talks
to these special little princes and princesses
who never asked to be
highlighting their strengths
and strengthening their weaknesses
helping them overcome being the special needs student
eventually, becoming
Superheroes too

cleaning up their own mistakes and messes
celebrating every goal milestone, big or small
partying with purpose

you give students choice, and voice
well versed in functional skills, self-contained
and instructional resource
in the *Least Restrictive Environment*
you provide a
Free Appropriate Public Education

God's Special Educators Are Teachers Too

to all, honoring the
Individuals with Disabilities Education Act

Super teachers push goal reachers
and make super readers

although, seldom recognized for your sacrifice
God has a special place for you
because God's Special educators are teachers too

Jeanine Jones

N-Z Poetic Inspiration for God's Special Educator

Jeanine Jones

Negotiator...

Negotiating assignment choices, contracts
and the behavior plan, which is non-negotiable
you make the sweetest deals
offering the gift of education
to little learners

you give
they take and you don't seem to mind
knowing that it will all pay off
in due time

as head negotiator
you delegate attendance runners
line leaders, hall monitors, clipboard holders
white board washers, class representatives
speakers, announcement makers
pencil sharpeners, delegators
and junior negotiators

filling all the class jobs weekly
so that everyone gets a turn
equity helps your students
buy into what they need to learn

mediating class conflicts diplomatically
you referee fairly and free
going between "gum in her hair" issues
to "he took my pencil" blues

since classroom management is your suit
all issues are diffused
and back to the normalcy of teaching you go
your negotiating tactics pay off and...

the nuggets you deposit daily
are revealed in quizzes, test and performance task
deeming you the best negotiator
I mean teacher of all time

Optimistic...

Optimistically, believing
you can do anything
you challenge scholars to reach for horizons
beyond the stars, sunsets and sunrises
beyond moons: crescent, lunar, gibbous, quarter, half and
full

making them believe that they can do anything
astronomically thinking they can reach galaxies...
out of this world

going the distance with no limits
leaving your presence and space...
as engineers and astronauts

ready to launch

Preparer...

Preparer of many things

making lists of preparation in your "me time"
has prepared you for a special place
with a winning admittance ticket

everything from group names, décor, supplies
and possible class pets
appear on the August, September, fall lists

cursive alphabet tape
wipes, plants, fish, bird, crates
all the things that have to be done before the first day
for the first day of school fun

welcome message on the board and letter to parents
introductory games
puzzles with your new students names
all about you and readers interest surveys
routine, schedules, class rules and norms

supplies, supplies, supplies

room tour, idea list, greetings at the door
leading star scholars

to the walk the red carpet on the floor
pictures, grade level packets, warm ups
announcements, announcements, announcements
book trailer and read-aloud

you pencil in belt and shoes
and other things on your personal list
you need to do for your own kid
to be ready for school

checking off books and rotations
you begin the tasks
of how you will manage stations

then moving on to the tasks on your next list
carefully placing ABC's, number operations, site words
transition words, accountable talk stems and name strips
on rearranged desks

you go home, try to rest and refresh for tomorrow
the first day of school

after the first day, you print pictures, regroup
realizing you have to start on your new list
to prepare this year's set of students
for greatness!

Jeanine Jones

Quintessential...

Setting high standards
you are the ideal role model
essential, prototypical, and original
classic, not your typical teacher

propelling your students to...

revolve like the earth
blow like the wind
set sparks like fire
freely flow like water

into the world

that is theirs for the taking
you are the essence
of an exemplary educator

Resourceful...

Paving a road to academic stardom
from the bottom up

utilizing everything you have
to access young brains
and make a concept
come to life
for your scholars

using tools, unlimited resources, materials and supplies
stretching quantities to deliver new information and skills

never compromising
the quality of education
quick-witted and resourceful
you empower others
and make learning and teaching
powerful

Special...

Not your average educator

different in the way you handle your class
with class, you reign exceptionally superior

under your special teachings
shiny little superstars go far
reaching for their individual goals

your passion for education
and for taking others further
is undeniable

you are truly God's special educator

Tenacious...

With the tenacity of a parent in a teacher's role
in full swing, no-nonsense mode

your insistent firmness and tough love
keeps the students in control

considering you may be the only constant in a child's life
you often turn shortcomings
into success
under your steadfast hold
students often transition from failing
to being the best

some call you mean
and say your class is hard
but are most thankful for the solid start...
to venture out into the reality
of the real tough world

Unique...

In your unique
distinct teacher voice
you command attention during roll call
and lesson presentations

when you walk into the room
students assume the position of learning

sometimes your hair is a little disheveled
your colorful eyeglass frames
compliment your free spirit style of dress
although, you never try to impress fashion wise
your focus is to impress their minds
never allowing students to be dismissed
with blank canvases

you are an artist
your room is an art space
promoting...
Creative Learning in a Unique Environment
for young artist to landscape their ideas
and make bold statements

Versatile...

You're admired for your versatility
versatile is your middle name
Magician Versatile More

adapting to whatever situation the day brings
like a true professional
having many talents
you had to be sent from heaven
to train little darlings and angels
to run the world and get the nation on track

and make America what it never was

figuratively changing hats and bags
like models change clothes
for your multipurpose role

as teacher extraordinaire

Wonder...

Incredible in everyway
you make wonderful things happen everyday
creating a wondrous world of wonders
phenomenally blowing minds with new information
wonderfully working your magic
one wiz at a time

students enter your world of wonder
and get all of their why questions answered
through evaluation, problem solving and process of
elimination
your wonderful work is everlasting

Xenial...

Most xenial since the first day
of the year's learning

letting students make their new classroom
their home
hospitably, welcoming them to their learning abode

teaching your newest group of little friends
how be to be social, respectful and smart

from the beginning
when you cheered in your own student friendly way

Ready, set, start!

you set a warm tone for learning

Yippee...

Finally!
You made it!
all year you've counted down
from 180 days to now
you've worked so hard
from the very start

teaching, counseling and coaching

your students have taken all you have
many days you thought about grabbing your coat
and all your bags

at this time, it's safe to release a big

YIPPEE!

Hip, hip, hooray

the last day of school
is quickly approaching

Zappy...

Eye catching and lively as you enter the room
is your teacher status

zappy, happy energy is what you bring
zapping out students fears and doubts

trusting that they can achieve all of their dreams and hopes
the vibes of positivity and possibility
you've instilled in your scholars is commendable

bow...

you deserve the teacher of the year award

Thank you for reading!

Jeanine Jones

Read all the books in the...
An Alphabet Soup Bowl in a Book Series

When All God's Teachers Get To Heaven

God's Special Educators are Teachers Too

Librarians LOL

Teachers LOL

Doing 180 Days to Life

ABOUT THE AUTHOR

Jeanine Jones, born Jeanine Books, is a native of Chicago, Illinois. As an educator in an urban school system, she is responsible for educating youth who are challenged in the areas of academics and socio-economics. Cultural development, the arts and literacy are important factors in her work. She is continuously striving to develop new strategies that are effective for struggling readers. Her absolute affinity for literature, especially poetry, propels her to teach and constantly learn. As a spoken-word artist, poet, and creative writer, Arts Integration is an essential component of her practice. She attributes her early love of reading and the arts to her parents. They made it possible for her to experience and live life creatively.

"Literacy is Life~ Live!" is her motto.

www.ingramcontent.com/pod-product-compliance
Lightning Source LLC
Chambersburg PA
CBHW071635040426
42452CB00009B/1643